Forgotten faces of
Swansea

By David Roberts

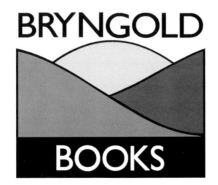

BRYNGOLD
BOOKS

First published in Great Britain in 2009 by
Bryngold Books Ltd.,
Golden Oaks, 98 Brynau Wood, Cimla,
Neath, South Wales, SA11 3YQ.
www.bryngoldbooks.com

Typesetting, layout,
editing and design
by Bryngold Books

ISBN 978-1-905900-14-5

Printed and bound
in Wales by
Gomer Press,
Llandysul, Ceredigion.

Contents

Appreciation

I am indeted to so many people for their help and encouragement in the production of *Forgotten Faces of Swansea*. My thanks in particular are due to the Lord Mayor of Swansea, Councillor Alan Lloyd, for kindly contributing the foreword.

The book itself would not have been possible without the support of people from far and wide who have shared their pictures from the past to produce a fascinating record for future generations. These include Ray & Dorothy Lewis who once again supplied an array of fascinting and atmospheric images, Barry Griffiths, Steve Davies, Gaye Mortali, Betty Matthews, Marjorie Ball, James Ackland, Tony Ridler, Julia Bennett, Christine Rix, John Jones, Alan Lloyd, Clive Saddington, Colin Andrew, Norman Sullivan, Mel Clare, Ken Morse, Madge Johns, Jean Evans, Anthony Hughes, Gloria Wilson, Helen Smith, Julie Jones, TB Harris, Bill Bateman, Terry & Joy Osborn, Steve Phillips, Bernard Humphries, Dennis Spinks, Pamela Parkhill, Bert Barton, Mrs PA Davies, Rev Roy Bevan, Clive Williams, Robin Wayne, WG Humphreys, Clive Cockings, Don Roberts, Jodie Jones, Sandra Walters, Angela Bailey, Pam Evans, Carolyn Harris, Hazel Rees, John & Marian Murphy, David Lile, Bill Davies, Keith Taylor, Rita Henry, Sandra Hayden, Royston Morgan, Mrs Hilary Isaac, Jim Davies, The late Alan Jones, William Bateman, Rhoda E Davies, Roger Evans, Alan Giffard, Mervyn Roberts, Hilary Evans, David and Eiluned Govier, Alan Williams, Malcolm Williams, Richard Baglow, John & Barbara Southard, Rita Lewis, Tony James and Andrew Hinton. Others without whose help the book would not have appeared incude David Beynon, Gerald Gabb, Bernard Morris, Anthony Isaac and Neil Melbourne.

Finally, I must salute the patience and assistance of my wife Cheryl who, to date, has been my guiding light in a journey that has seen the compilation of no fewer than 23 books. By now she probably knows the route better than me.

Share your pictures!

If you would like to play a part in recording the history of Swansea by contributing photographs to the next nostalgia book in this successful series please telephone 01639 643961
or e-mail bryngold@btinternet.com to find out the ways in which you can do so. We would be delighted to hear from you.
All photographs — black and white or colour — of people, places, events, streets, buildings, schooldays and sport are considered whatever their age, subject or format. They are all promptly returned.
Also, if you have missed any of the previous books why not contact us now. You can also check out our website at
www.bryngoldbooks.com for details of other fascinating local nostalgia books.

Foreword

Like many other Swansea residents I have eagerly collected all of the previous editions of David Roberts' excellent books so I am delighted to have the opportunity to contribute the foreword for this latest volume. Amazingly it is the twelfth he has put together in consecutive years. That in itself is a tribute to his diligence and determination to help ensure that we will always have a record of the way we once were. Forgotten Faces of Swansea is a unique photographic flashback of the people and places of our city and county as well as our lives. Much more than that, it reflects the changing social scene of our own special slice of Wales.

David would tell you that he couldn't produce his books without the ongoing support of the residents of Swansea and indeed the many exiles who send him pictures. By the people, for the people is his favourite saying. We must however recognise his part in the scheme of things. Without his time and energy Swansea wouldn't have such a worthwhile annual album that is so readily accessible to so many.

This wonderful series of books bridges the gap between the generations and lets us all marvel at the changing fashions and wonder at the different social trends. Everybody is fascinated by the structural changes that have occurred over the passage of time. Changes that often quietly pass us by. It is so enjoyable to savour the

atmosphere and memories that every photograph evokes. They say a picture is worth a thousand words — if that is the case then Forgotten Faces of Swansea and those books before it say a great deal about our lives and the communities in which we live. I wish David well with his latest publication and look forward to seeing the 'new' old photos that bring memories flooding back. Perhaps even more importantly I would encourage everyone to sift through their photographs of people, places and events, not just from decades back, but closer to the present time, and keep on providing David with the material he continually needs to ensure that his books remain such a welcome highlight in the Swansea calendar.

Councillor Alan Lloyd,
Lord Mayor,
City & County of Swansea.

Second city firsts

This year marks a significant anniversary in the history of Swansea. It is 40 years since the proud town assumed the prestigious mantle of city status. When His Royal Highness Prince Charles, just days into his new role as Prince of Wales, stood on the steps of the Guildhall and conferred the title on the city it marked the beginning of another new era.

Much of the way Swansea, Wales' second city, was before — and since — that memorable milestone is evidenced by the many images reproduced on the pages of Forgotten Faces of Swansea. They show that the city and its people are never slow to grasp an opportunity.

Swansea has always been at the forefront of industrial and technical development. It was, for example, the first location in Wales to have electric tramcars. It was also the first to screen moving pictures for the masses.

Much has changed since the city's determined quest to be one of the best as it emerged from the ashes of wartime destruction was given a well-deserved boost on that gloriously sunny July day in 1969. The city has blazed a trail in which others have followed. It created the first major river barrage, the first new maritime quarter from old dockland, the first major indoor tennis centre and the first and largest Enterprise Zone in Britain. The Quadrant Shopping Centre was one of the most modern in Wales at the time it was built.

The lower Swansea Valley, once a polluted, industrial wasteland, has blossomed forth again with both greenery and commerce. Even before the building of the new Liberty Stadium for the Swans and the Ospreys, the Morfa Stadium which was there before was one of the most modern running tracks and sports centres in the UK. Now the SA1 dockland revival has resulted in a vibrant, new part of the city which will soon be home to another marina. The Waterfront museum and leisure centre are additional key projects.

Some city scenes have changed little in 40 years while others have altered out of all recognition. Yet still more will undergo development as the Century rolls on. Perhaps that is ample reason to treasure the look back in time that this book offers. While the city moves forward it allows us to refresh our memories of the way it once was.

David Roberts,
2009

Two South Wales Transport buses — one bound for Sketty, the other Langland Bay, dominate this view along Oxford Street towards Castle Buildings, 1950. Beside them is the impressive entrance to Swansea Market.

Street Scene

The majestic sweep of Swansea Bay as it appeared from Pantycelyn Road in August 1966.

The entrance to Swansea Infirmary, at the junction of St Helen's Road and Brynymor Road, 1900.

The pavements in Oxford Street were bustling with shoppers when this early 1900s summertime picture was taken.

A tram car heads along St Helen's Road, 1908.

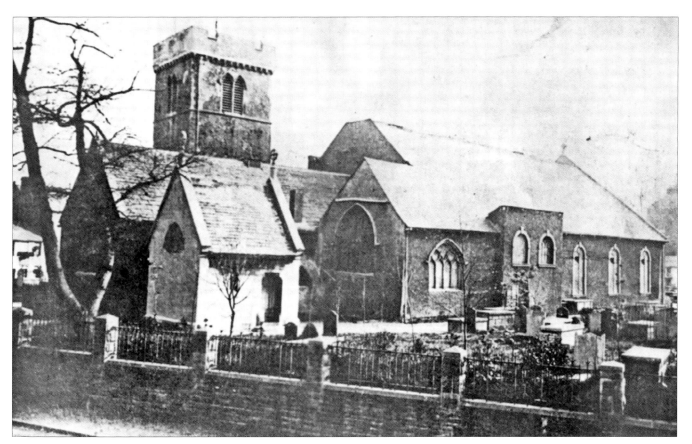

Old St Mary's Church, 1888.

Island House dominates
this view of Wind Street,
taken about 1878.
Within two years the
building had been
demolished.

Crowds leaving the Mumbles train at Rutland Street terminus, early 1900s.

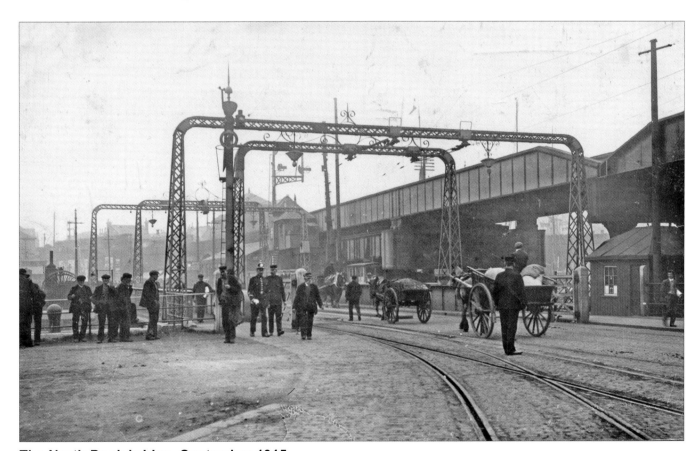

The North Dock bridge, September 1915.

The impressive entrance to Swansea market dominates this view westward along
Oxford Street, 1912.

Castle Street, looking towards High Street, 1920.

York Street was a hive of activity when this 1908 scene was captured. These keen motorists converged on Acklands garage before setting off on a rally. The chapel in the centre background is still there today.

The New Cut swing bridge which spanned the River Tawe, 1933.

Swansea Market, Oxford Street, late 1930s. It was erected in 1897 and destroyed in the wartime blitz of February, 1941. The building's distinctive roof can clearly be seen.

The Carlton Cinema, late 1930s.

St Mary's Church after the
Three Nights' Blitz,
February, 1941.

Properties in
Craddock
Street, 1934.

Owner Sid Ackland with staff and perhaps some customers outside Acklands Motor Garage at the lower end of Wind Street, late 1930s.

A South Wales Transport AEC Renown single deck bus turns into High Street from Alexandra Road, 1950.

Looking into Portland Street from the Kingsway, mid-1950s. The corner of the building alongside the car is where the Kardomah cafe is situated today.

Two youngsters pose for the photographer in Plymouth Street with Oxford Street behind them, March 1950. Many will remember Samuel Clompus's antique shop on the left.

Looking up Princess Way, mid-1950s.

An early 1950's view of Swansea's town centre.

The new nave of St Mary's Parish Church, looking west, shortly before its official re-opening, 1959.

Swansea's distinctive Guildhall at dusk in August 1965.

A policeman controls traffic at the junction of Alexandra Road and High Street. The railings behind him surrounded the entrance to underground toilets,1960s.

High Street at its junction with College Street, 1961. Woolworth's and its cafeteria are on the right.

Looking into town across Swansea's New Cut swing bridge, early 1960s.

York Street, late 1960s.

Removing the high level railway bridge at the junction of Victoria Road and York Street, 1967.

A close-up of the attractive Castle Gardens fountain, summer 1970.

Vessels moored at the South Dock, July 1967.

Looking down on Port Tennant and a busy Swansea Docks, 1969.

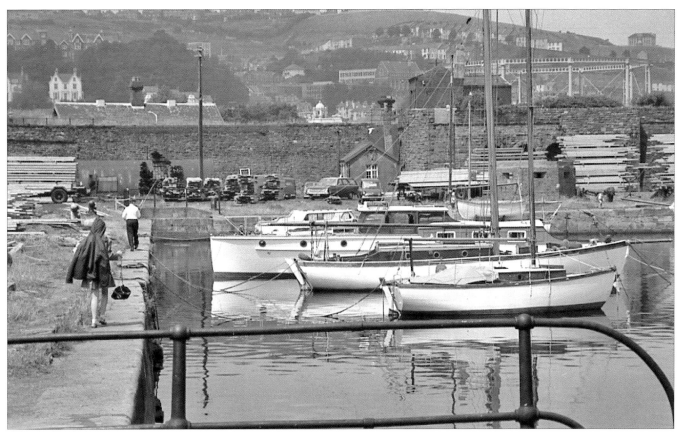

A view across the western end of the South Dock, July 1967.

An early 1970s panorama of central Swansea with the unmistakable arched glass roof of the market commanding centre stage.

Oystermouth Road, August 1974. The terraced properties in the centre have been boarded up prior to demolition.

Oystermouth Road endured far less traffic in 1974 when this picture was taken. Quadruple Green Shield stamps were used to lure motorists to the filling station on the left.

A bird's eye view of some of the buildings that caught the eye at the eastern gateway to Swansea in 1969, the year it finally achieved city status.

Looking up Dillwyn Street, from its junction with Singletion Street, 1976.

Oxford Street at it junction with Dilwyn Street, August 1976. The building on the right is Oxford Street School.

Singleton Street bus station, 1976.

Looking along Oystermouth Road towards the city centre, 1976.

Low tide near the entrance to the South Dock basin before work started on construction of the River Tawe barrage, 1979.

Refurbishing cobbled Constitution Hill, mid 1980s.

A City Mini bus turns into Caer Street with Castle Gardens on the left and the revamped BT Tower dwarfing the ruins of Swansea Castle, behind, 1988.

The Queens Hotel, Gloucester Place, 1989.

A bird's eye view of the former Royal Mail depot at The Strand from the ninth floor of its Telecom Tower neighbour, 1988.

Looking across Castle Gardens into Caer Street and beyond it, St Mary's Church, early 1980s.

The Telecom tower seen
from the entrance to Castle
Lane, 1976. Swansea castle
remains are on the left.

Vessels moored in the River Tawe on the seaward side of New Cut bridge before construction of the barrage, 1986.

The Kingsway, busy with traffic, 1988.

Looking landward across the South Dock, 1990.

The view across Swansea's eastside from the ninth floor of the Telecom tower during work to clad its exterior with a mirror-like finish, 1988.

The unusual facade of the Welsh Glass Works company's building, Quay Parade, 1989.

The former Swansea Guildhall, Somerset Place, before it was restored to its current glory as the Dylan Thomas Centre, 1990.

Work underway on road improvements at the junction of The Kingsway and Princess Way, 2006. The former pedestrian underpass was filled in during the project.

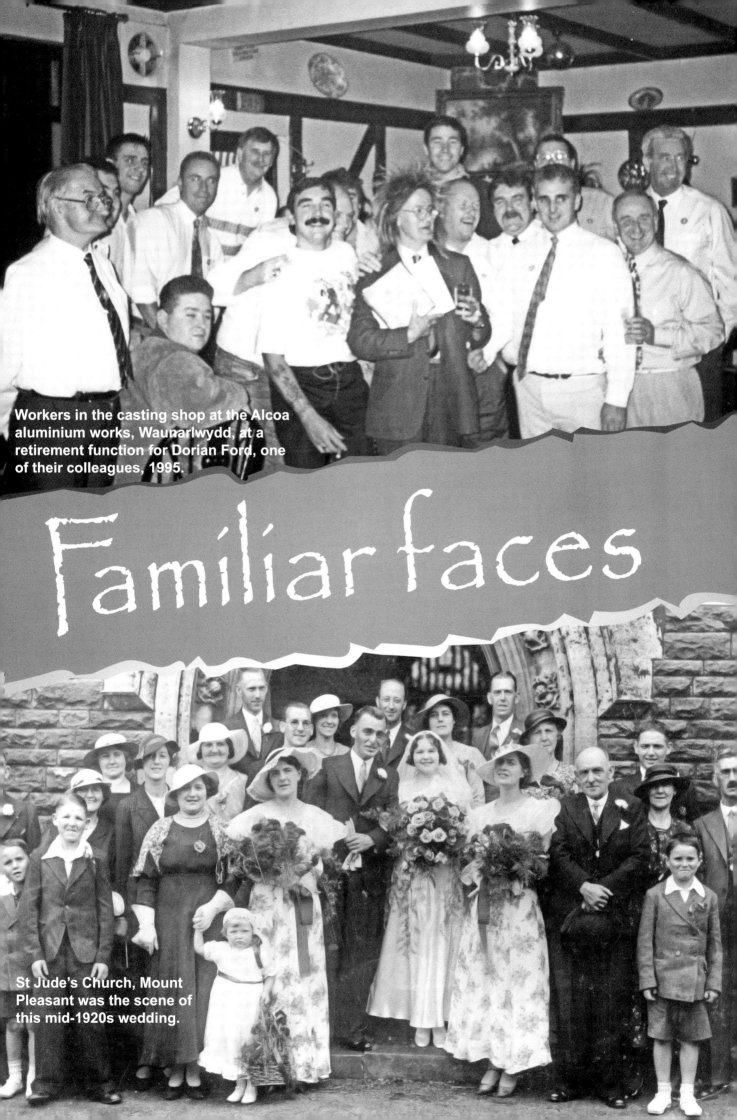

Workers in the casting shop at the Alcoa aluminium works, Waunarlwydd, at a retirement function for Dorian Ford, one of their colleagues, 1995.

Familiar faces

St Jude's Church, Mount Pleasant was the scene of this mid-1920s wedding.

One for the album! This gathering consisted of members of the Maddocks family from Hafod. All dressed up in their best outfits they had visited a photographic studio for this picture in 1935.

Madge and Gordon John, with the guests who helped celebrate their marriage, all pictured in the garden of a house at Nicander Parade, Mayhill, 1944.

Members of the Home Guard detachment who manned the Second World War rocket battery at Ashleigh Road, 1944.

Members of the youth club which was held at the back of Church House, a hostel for clergymen in St Helen's Road, 1944.

Members of the St Helen's area
Mothers' Union at Sandfields Church,
early 1950s.

Sketty Brownies provide a
guard of honour at a local
wedding, possibly that of their
Brown Owl, 1949.

Some of the members of Christ Church Youth Club,
Oystermouth Road, 1945.

The successful womens' darts team of the Jersey Arms public house, Neath Road, Hafod, mid-
1950s. Behind them are some of their male counterparts.

The official annual Christmas photograph taken of staff at the Swansea office of the Liverpool Victoria Friendly Society, early 1950s.

Members of St Thomas Church Sunday School, October 1965.

Members of Swansea Council's Health Committee with the Mayor, Councillor Arthur Reed, 1970.

A proud moment for one young Swansea girl as she hands over a posy of flowers to a special guest at a function at the city's YMCA, December 7, 1972.

A friends night out in the Red Cow public house, Waun Wen, 1953.

Swansea Superintendent Registrar Cyril Bowlie welcomes Prime Minister Edward Heath during his visit to Swansea, 1972.

Sandfields Mother's Union church group pictured with civic dignitaries and guests during a function held in the early 1950s.

Some of the members who attended the opening of Dunvant Rugby Club's new premises during the early 1970s.

Swansea's successful Its A Knockout competition team shortly before heading off to Maastricht to represent the UK in 1975. They were given a civic send off by Mayoress Councillor Peggy Morgan and other civic representatives.

Directors and staff of the JT Morgan warehouse at an annual Christmas party in the 1970s.

Members of the Swansea and West Wales Airport Consortium at their final meeting, March 15, 1974.

The new Welsh and Swansea presidents of the Christian Endeavour Society sign the visitors book at the Lord Mayor's parlour, 1980.

Members of Swansea Christian Endeavour Society's committee, at the inception of a new president, early 1980s.

Lord Mayor of Swansea, Councillor Howard Morgan, with Her Majesty the Queen and Prince Philip at the official opening of Morfa Athletic Stadium, 1980. It was demolished in 1999 and later replaced by the Liberty Stadium which opened on July 10, 2005.

Staff at South Wales Transport's Ravenhill garage gather to salute the retirement of a colleague during the early 1960s.

Nine members of the 1st Swansea, Fforestfach, Brownie Pack, 1983.

Staff of Debenhams department store at a Christmas celebration, 1985.

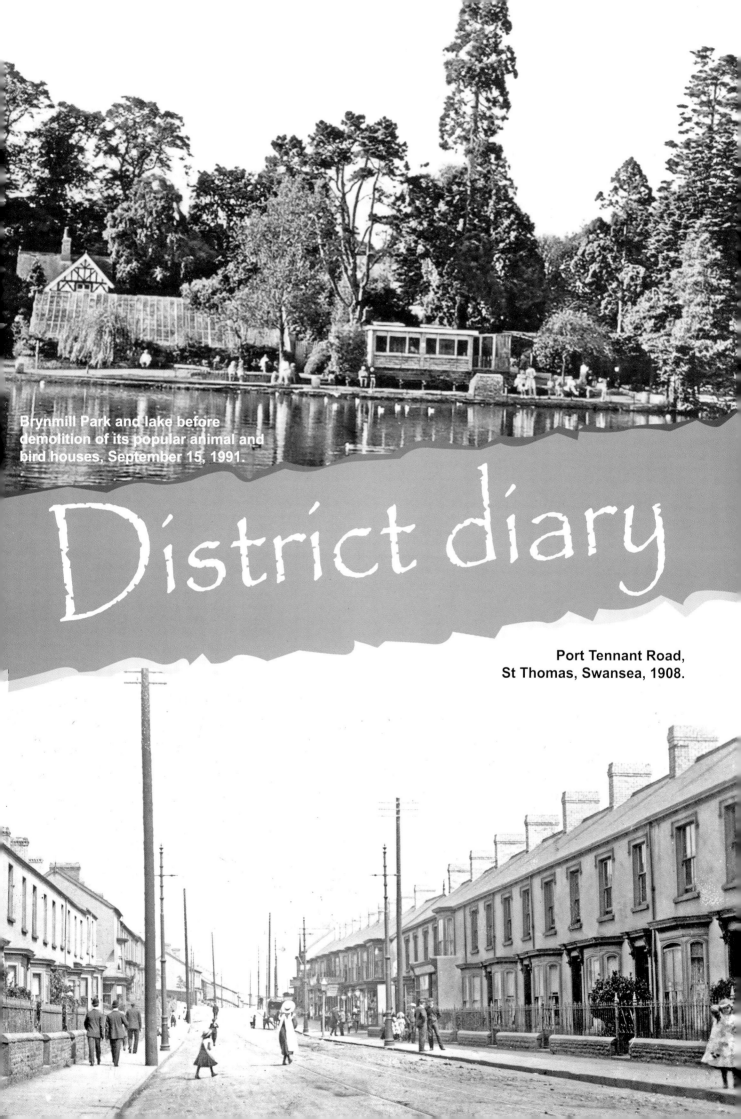

Brynmill Park and lake before demolition of its popular animal and bird houses, September 15, 1991.

District diary

Port Tennant Road,
St Thomas, Swansea, 1908.

Bryn Newydd, Llangyfelach Road, Treboeth, 1905. In its time the house served many uses before becoming the Pines Country Club. This closed on December 31, 2007.

A tram nears its terminus at Bryn Road, Brynmill, 1905.

Looking down Gower Road towards Sketty Cross, 1912.

Eversley Road, Sketty, 1912.

Over the top at Limeslade. A scene much different today. This motorist had a lucky escape when his car rolled through the fence, 1912.

REFRESHMENTS

Looking up Church Street, Morriston, 1930. St John's Church is in the background.

Birchgrove Road, Birchgrove, late 1930s.

Morriston railway station and goods yard, 1930.

The Patti Pavilion and flower beds in Victoria Park, 1936.

A steam-powered lorry heads down Waunarlwydd Road into the square at Cockett, mid-1930s. Cefn Coed Hospital is in the background.

The railway viaduct over the River Tawe at Landore with a workmens cradle underneath, 1958.

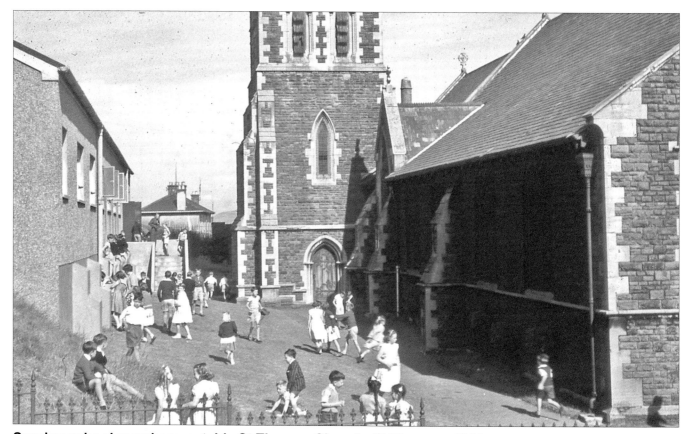

Sunday school members outside St Thomas Church, St Thomas, 1963.

Looking towards heavily industrialised Bynea over the road bridge that crossed the River Loughor in the early 1950s. Built in 1923, it linked western Swansea and Llanelli. It was replaced by a new bridge in the 1990s.

The old cottage around which the sprawling Ravenhill depot and workshops of the South Wales Transport bus company was built, 1955.

An atmospheric image of a milk float almost marooned in unseasonal snow at Bryn Newydd Gardens, Sketty Green, April 14, 1966.

Carmarthen Road at its junction with Convent Street above Dyffaty Cross, 1975.

A view of the St Thomas railway station site from Windmill Terrace, November 30, 1982.

Terraced homes in Calland Street, Plasmarl, 1976.

The sign says it all! Construction work underway on the studios of Swansea Sound at Victoria Road, Gowerton, 1973. The station began broadcasting on September 30, 1974.

Nantyffin Road, Llansamlet, near the main Swansea to Paddington railway line, August 1972.

Looking towards Mount Pleasant from Kilvey Hill, late 1960s. The Palace Theatre is dwarfed by Dyfatty flats.

A band entertains visitors in picturesque Clyne Gardens, May 23, 1993.

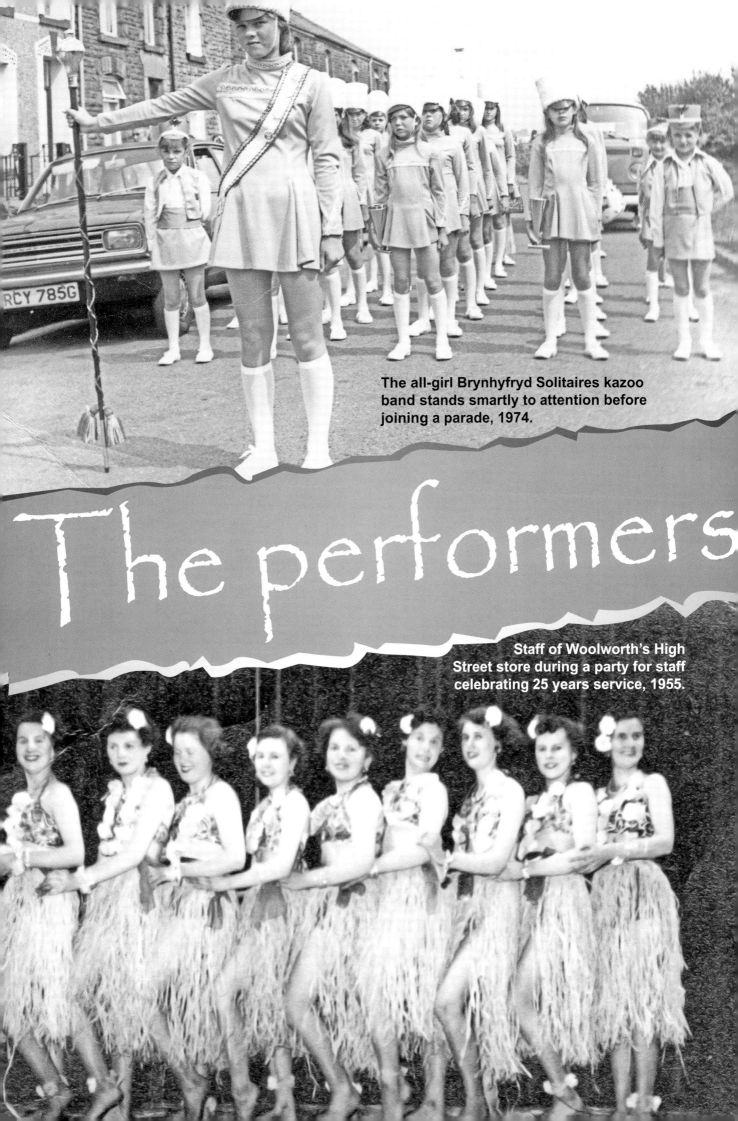

The all-girl Brynhyfryd Solitaires kazoo band stands smartly to attention before joining a parade, 1974.

The performers

Staff of Woolworth's High Street store during a party for staff celebrating 25 years service, 1955.

With their teacher Miss Phillips are pupils of Terrace Road Primary School who formed a dance team that competed against other schools across Swansea at Vetch Field, 1944.

The Swansea Police band playing at St.Helen's sports ground, late 1950's.

A popular dance class organised by Rae and Jim Copp at St David's Church Hall, 1948.

Members of the cast of Miranda, a play staged by the dramatic society of St Michael's Church, Manselton, 1960.

Gaily dressed participants in a concert staged by Waunarlwydd Women's Institute, late 1960s.

Producer David Thomas puts some of the cast through their paces during rehearsals for Uplands Arts Club's Silver Jubilee year performance of The Mikado, 1967.

Members of Morriston Orpheus Choir outside the Ivor Sims Memorial Hall, formerly Nazareth Chapel, Morriston in 1977 before departing for the Berlin Military Tattoo in honour of the Queen's Silver Jubilee. The choir sang to capacity audiences at each of its performances in West Berlin.

Three members of the Hazel Johnson School of Dance rehearse their moves in readiness for a dance festival at Craig-y-Nos, 1976.

Young members of the Hazel Johnson School of Dance rehearse a routine at Penlan Community Centre, mid-1980s.

The cast of the Nativity Play staged at Carmarthen Road United Reformed Church, Greenhill, 1981.

Boys of the Hazel Johnson School of Dance as the Bad Boys in a charity concert at Penllergaer village hall, 1981.

South Wales Evening Post editor Nick Carter addresses the audience after a performance by the talented cast of the Bumbles of Mumbles concert on stage at the Grand Theatre, 1987, while organiser Alex Frith proudly looks on.

The cast of The Grand Theatre pantomime, Snow White and the Seven Dwarfs, with Lord Mayor, Colin Hammacott, outside the Mansion House, 1991. Among them was Linda Lusardi, Stu Francis, Neil Morrisey, Owen Money, Mike Holloway, Nikki Kelly and The Mini Tones.

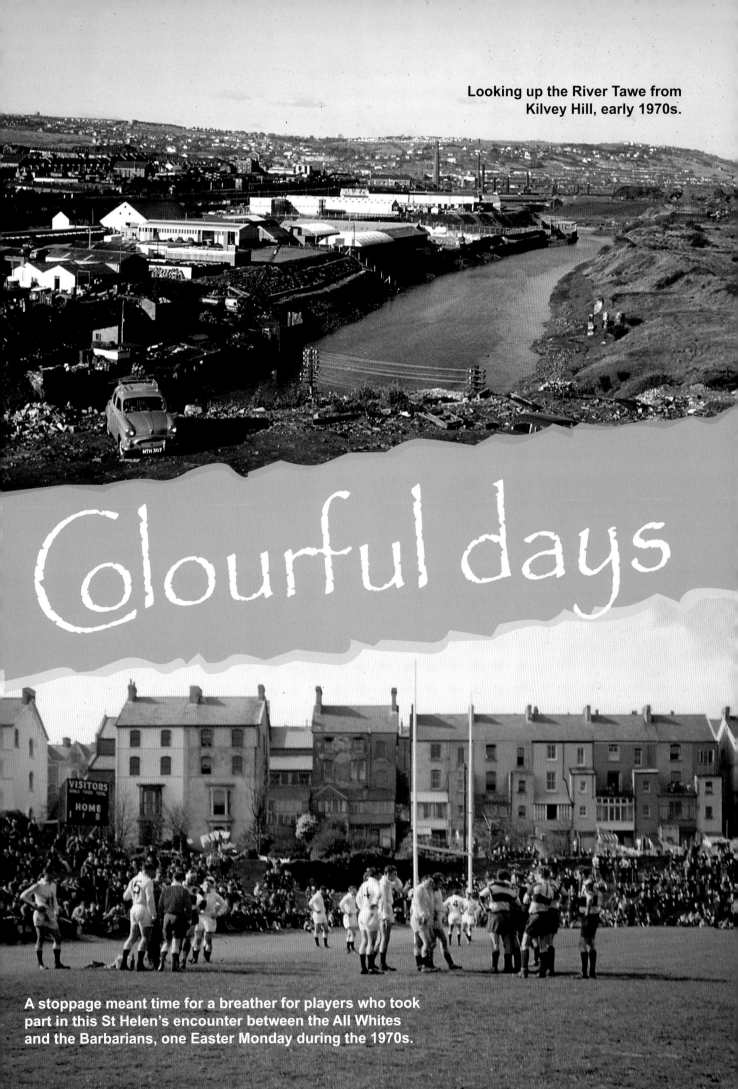

Looking up the River Tawe from Kilvey Hill, early 1970s.

Colourful days

A stoppage meant time for a breather for players who took part in this St Helen's encounter between the All Whites and the Barbarians, one Easter Monday during the 1970s.

These young pupils of The Bryn Nursery wore fancy dress at a farewell party for one of its teachers, April, 1988. The nursery was closed at the end of the summer term, July 2006.

Powys Avenue, Townhill football team, 1970s.

Young bathers enjoy the sun, sand and sea at Langland Bay, August 3, 1974.

Past members of staff from Plasmarl Post Office returned there to celebrate the retirement after 30 years service of the current owner in 1996.

One of West Glamorgan Fire Services specialist tenders, 1991.

The interior of Clyne Chapel, 1972.

Gas holders alongside Oystermouth Road, July 26, 1989. Today the site is home to Tesco's Marina supermarket.

This South Wales Transport ble decker was painted as a ub to celebrate 100 years of Truman's ales in the 1970s.

TRUMAN

WELCOME

Teaching staff at Arfryn Primary School, Heol Frank, Penlan, 1994.

Weaver's grain store and dock basin, Quay Parade, 1969.

WEAVER & COMPANY LIMITED

WEAVER &

CORK FERRY

SOLD

DANGER

Plantasia, Swansea's botanical gem, 1990.

A novel way to see the city. The winter fair big wheel, 2007.

The former Norwegian Seamen's Mission that stood alongside the River Tawe, 1990. At the start of the SA1 redevelopment it was dismantled and rebuilt a short distance away.

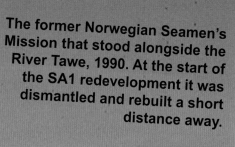

Looking up towards Singleton Street and Dilwyn Street, 1988.

A fascinating view of
Manselton Park, 1908.

Beach huts at
Rotherslade,
August ,1989.

Bandsmen of the Welsh Guards lead a detachment of their comrades onto St Helen's Road during a parade through Swansea in September 1982.

WILKS MUSIC STORES

First Communion of children at Holy Cross Church, Gendros with Father, now Canon, Flook, May 1998.

Oasis Park was the forerunner of today's Parc Tawe retail complex. This is one of the entrances in 1990.

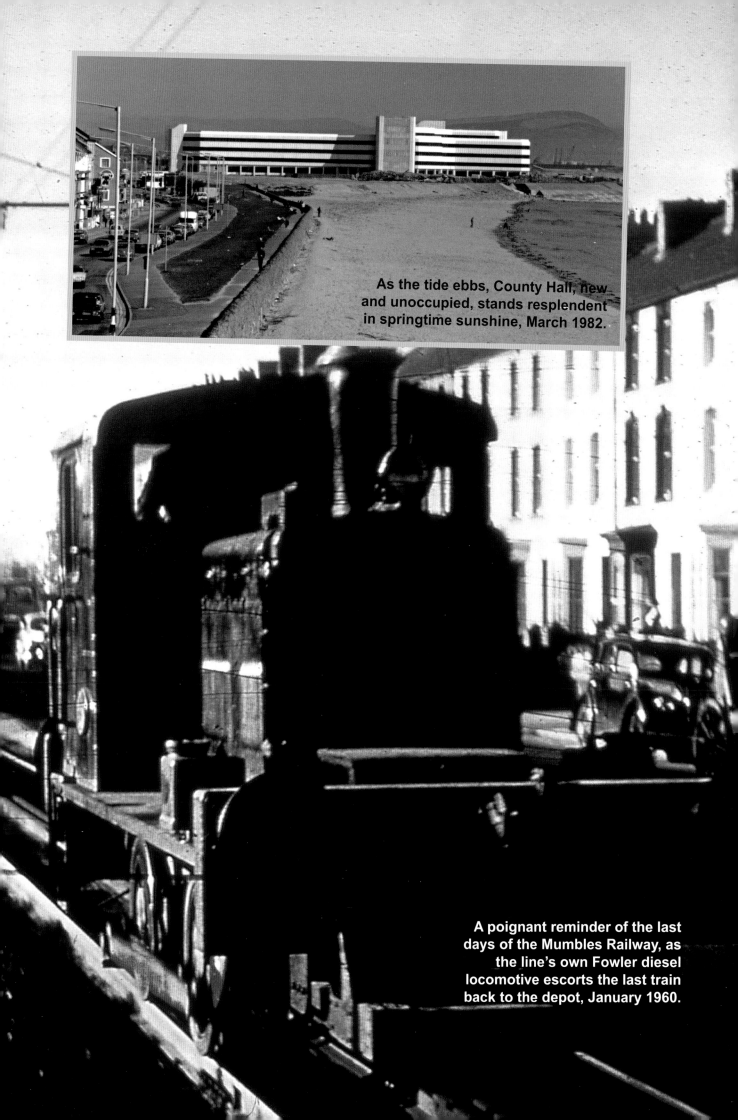

As the tide ebbs, County Hall, new and unoccupied, stands resplendent in springtime sunshine, March 1982.

A poignant reminder of the last days of the Mumbles Railway, as the line's own Fowler diesel locomotive escorts the last train back to the depot, January 1960.

Entrants line up for the judge in one of the sections of the goat classes at the Gower Show at Fairwood, August 4, 1988.

Crowds at the City of Swansea Show, Singleton Park, August 30, 1993.

The assembly area for the Corgi and Corgi Junior toys at the company's Fforestfach factory, 1983.

Making waves on Blackpill boating lake, August 16, 1969.

Langland Bay with its ranks of bathing huts on a sunny day, September 4, 1991.

Young entrants in one of the riding classes at the Gower Show at Fairwood, August 4, 1994.

Vehicles wait their turn at the traffic lights near The Slip bridge, March 29, 2003.

Cwmdonkin Park,
July 20, 1991.

93

Mumbles Carnival at Oystermouth Castle, July 27, 1995.

The terrace and garden at the Grand Theatre, 1990.

The impressive facade of the Grand Theatre, 1990.

Bustling Wind
Street, 1907.

Buying cockles
at Swansea Market,
July 26, 1989.

Looking across the
rooftops towards the River
Tawe and Swansea
Ferryport, early 1980s.

The Evening Post float that took part in the
Lord Mayor's Parade on May 23, 1992.

Construction
work underway
on the River Tawe
sail bridge,
April 5, 2003.

A panoramic view of the main
eastern traffic gateway into
Swansea, February 28, 1985.
It shows New Cut Bridge,
St Thomas and Kilvey Hill.

Princess Diana at St Helen's Sports Ground, February, 20 1992. She was visiting a Swansea primary schools' rugby display.

A popular Swansea market fish stall, July 1989.

The congregation of Bethel Welsh Chapel, Cockett, celebrating the Coronation of King George VI, May 12, 1937.

Parties & Parades

Residents of Beaufort Avenue, Kittle, celebrate the Investiture of Prince Charles as Prince of Wales, July, 1969.

Residents of Richardson Street during a party they held to celebrate the Coronation of King George VI, 1937.

A gathering of employees of Tom, Smith & Clark, chain manufacturers, New Cut Road, 1950.

Parents and children of Vivian Road, Sketty, during the street party they held to celebrate the Festival of Britain, June 1951.

Revellers at a Christmas dance organised by the staff of Richard Thomas and Baldwin's Pontardawe steelworks, 1952.

Sketty children in fancy dress to celebrate the Coronation of Queen Elizabeth II, June 1953.

These youngsters were in fancy dress as part of their street party in Cockett to celebrate the Coronation of Queen Elizabeth II, 1953.

Women workers at the Larma clothing factory at their Christmas party, 1959.

All smiles from these Sketty residents pictured with their children during Coronation celebrations, June 1953.

Marks and Spencer staff at their annual Christmas dinner dance, mid 1960s.

Guest cyclists at a Swansea Central Cycling Club dinner and dance, autumn 1955.

Staff of Campbell's furniture store, Oxford Street, at an annual dinner and dance, early 1950s.

Dilys and John Floyd of Morriston at the town's Swanmet Engineering Company's annual dinner and dance at the Dolphin Hotel, early 1950s.

Guests at the Swansea Coal Federation dance held in the Caswell Bay Hotel, 1962.

Demonstrators on the march in Swansea during the Cuban missile crisis of the 1960's. They are seen heading into Wind Street, with the Unifloc building in the background.

A group of employees and their partners celebrate New Year 1965 at the Gasworks Club.

A line-up of floats and participants in Mumbles carnival, at Bracelet Bay, before the start of the procession, July 30, 1983.

Staff of the Fisher Price division of Mettoy toy factory, Fforestfach, at their Christmas party, 1970.

The band of the Welsh Guards leads a parade to mark the Investiture of the Prince of Wales and his visit to Swansea, past the Guildhall, St Helen's, July 1969.

Morriston Militaires jazz band smartly leads
the way at a local carnival, 1978.

This was one of the floats that took part in Southgate Carnival, July 1971.

This motley crew took part in the Eastide Carnival in 1976. They are seen after the procession in Maesteg Park, St Thomas.

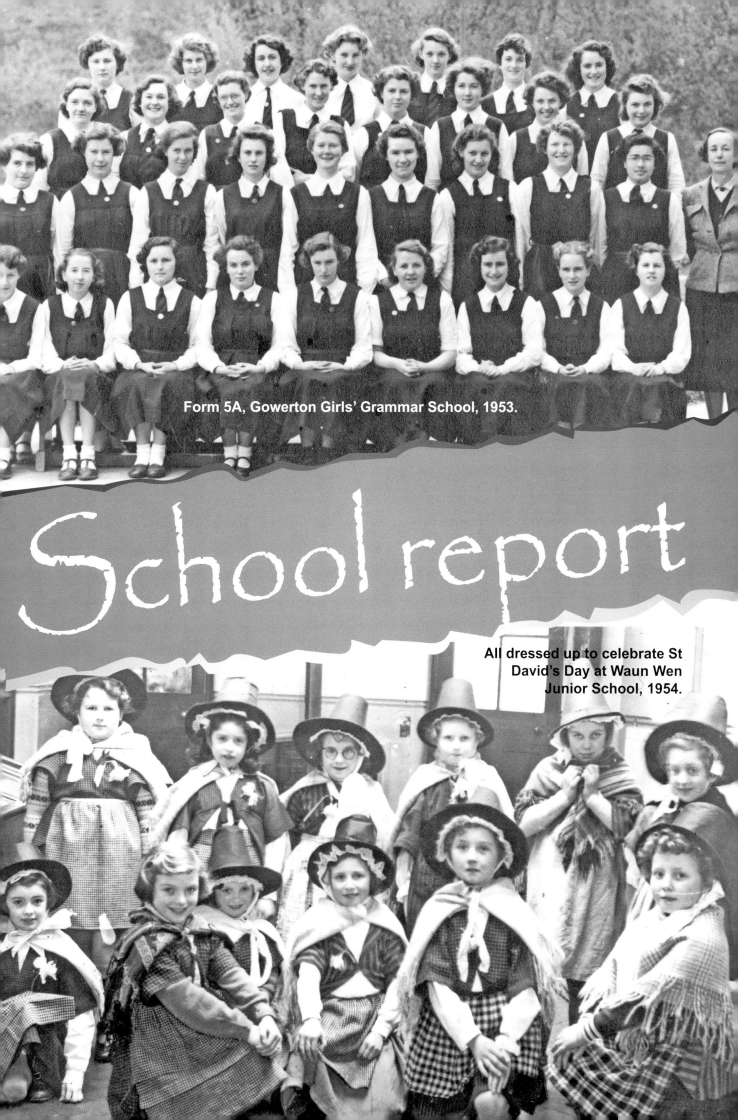

Form 5A, Gowerton Girls' Grammar School, 1953.

School report

All dressed up to celebrate St David's Day at Waun Wen Junior School, 1954.

Pupils of Oxford Street Girls Junior School with their teacher, 1917.

Pupils at Sketty Council School, 1911. Until 1909 they would have attended Sketty Church School in Gower Road which had served the village since the 1850s.

Oxford Street School pupils, 1917.

Class 2B, Morriston Infants School, with their teacher, 1920.

Pupils of Standard 1, Hendy Council Mixed School with their teacher and headteacher, 1920.

Pupils of Hafod Primary School, 1923.

All the pupils at Lloyd's School, 1949.

A class at St Helen's Boys School with their teacher Mr G Boyle, 1936.

A group of pupils at Glanmor School for Girls, 1955.

Some of the boys and girls who attended Waun Wen Junior School, 1949-50.

Sketty Primary School pupils, early 1950s.

A class of pupils at Oxford Street Boys Junior School with their teacher and headteacher, 1953.

Form 5C Dynevor Grammar School with teachers and headteacher, July 1954.

Pupils of Bishop Gore Grammar School, 1953.

A class at Sketty School, 1964.

Mrs O'Callagahan's class at Brynhyfryd Junior School with head teacher, Mr Gregory, late 1960s.

Tawe House, Terrace Road Primary School, 1971.

Pupils of class J3, Arfryn Primary School, Penlan with their teacher Mr Greenaway, 1972.

Pupils of Gorseinon Junior School with teachers, 1978.

One of the forms at Dynevor Grammar School with members of staff, 1963.

The nursery class at Stewart Hall, Sketty, spring term, 1972.

The Year 8 Creative Dancing team at Ysgol Gyfun Gwyr, 1988.

Girls at Gorseinon Infants School dressed in traditional costume on St David's Day, 1973.

Children at Nelson Terrace Nursery School, 1975. It was closed and subsequently demolished to make way for the building of the Quadrant Shopping Centre which opened in 1979.

A class at St Joseph's Infants School all dressed up for St David's Day celebrations, 1998.

Six-year old pupils at Parkland Primary School, Sketty, 1996.

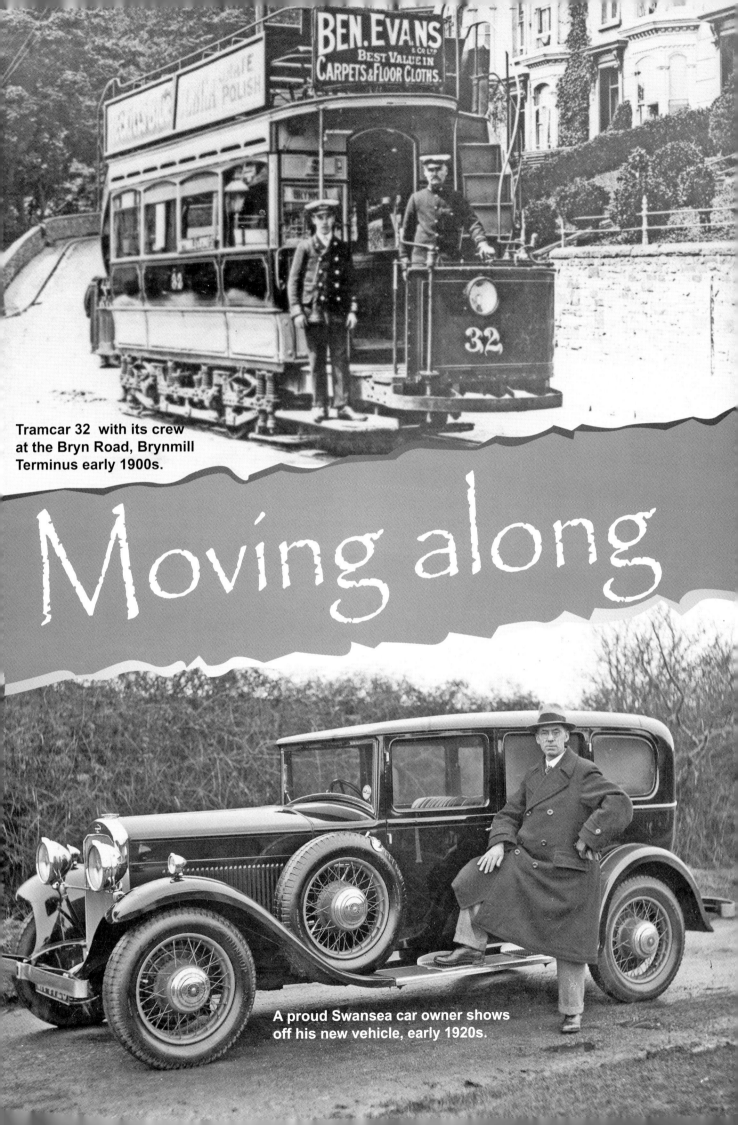

Tramcar 32 with its crew at the Bryn Road, Brynmill Terminus early 1900s.

Moving along

A proud Swansea car owner shows off his new vehicle, early 1920s.

The SS Fellside aground in Heatherslade Bay, Gower on January 8, 1924.

An AEC Renown demonstrator vehicle later bought by South Wales Transport for use on its Townhill route, late 1930s.

The SS Riverton entering Palmer's dry dock, Swansea after being torpedoed off St Ives in the Bristol Channel on April 23, 1945. She was towed there for repair and survived until 1969.

Wartime German submarines in Swansea Docks before being scrapped, 1946.

A De Havilland Dragon Rapide aircraft at Fairwood Common, during an air show, 1950.

Crowds at Fairwood Common during an air show, 1950.

A 1946 AEC Regent III South Wales Transport double deck bus with a 56 seat Weymann body. Buses like these carried thousands of passengers for the company during subsequent years.

Sid Ackland, left, of Ackland Motors with the Standard 10 car he drove with his brother in a Welsh Rally event in the early 1950s.

The lorry depot operated by British Road Services at North Dock, June 3, 1960. Inset: An 8-ton capacity Shelvoke & Drewry crane hoists aluminium slabs onto an eight-wheel Leyland vehicle ready for delivery to a customer in November of the same year.

A Leyland double decker together with two AEC vehicles in Castle Street, 1950. They were typical of buses operated by South Wales Transport in the years following the Second World War.

Taxis await their next fares outside High Street railway station, 1960.

Two British Road Services articulated lorries with drivers and staff at the company's North Dock depot, prepare to set off on their journey with large loads, 1961.

An array of different lorries await their next load at the British Road Services North Dock depot, November 6, 1960. Weaver's flour mill is behind. Today this is the site of the Parc Tawe retail complex.

The Balmoral pleasure steamer arriving at the South Dock entrance before construction of the River Tawe barrage, 1979.

Some of the fleet of Brian Isaac coaches at the company's garage at Mysydd Road, Landore — now a block of flats occupy the site — early 1980s.

The former Mumbles lifeboat, William Gammon, moored alongside Swansea Maritime and Industrial Museum, mid 1980s.

Mumbles lifeboat slides down the slipway and into the water, July 22, 1984.

The former Swansea pilot cutter Seamark moored at Swansea Docks, 1988.

Crowds enjoy the sun, sand and sea at Caswell Bay, 1975.

Break time

A family from Hafod enjoys time together on a Gower beach, 1917. The grandfather was on his first leave home from the Front during the First World War.

A family posing in their best beachwear during a summertime visit to Caswell Bay, late 1940s.

Cwmfelin steelworks employees on a day out, 1948.

Fishermen on Mumbles Pier, August 1970.

Employees from the Larma clothing factory enjoy a day out in Weston Super Mare, 1960.

Crowds throng Mumbles Pier, 1910. They are gathering to listen to a military band concert. Crowds appear to have gathered on the clifftop overlooking the pier too.

Two young women parade in their Sunday best, early 1920s. They are pictured draped in the fox fur stoles that were popular at the time.

Four Manselton women on a day out to Cheddar, Somerset, 1932.

Staff of tobacconists Davies & Price, who had a shop next door to Mount Pleasant Chapel, together with family and friends before setting out on a coach trip to the Elan Valley, mid-Wales, 1947.

A group of employees from Hodges clothing factory, Fforestfach, gather in Princess Way before setting off for a day trip, early 1950s.

Signwriters and coachbuilders employed by the South Wales Transport bus company in fancy dress on an outing in the late 1950s.

Porters Playboys were sure to have enjoyed themselves on this 1950s day out by coach.

British Home Stores staff on a visit to Chepstow, July 1958.

Quad bikes could be hired at
Blackpill lido, July 14, 1990.

Swansea's parks and entertainment centres often
offer a welcome break for residents. Here, members
of the city's Parks and Entertainment Committee are
pictured alongside Singleton Park boating lake
during their annual tour, 1968.

A family relaxes on the wall alongside Singleton Park boating lake, 1970.

Members of the congregation at St Joseph's Cathedral and surrounding parishes in the garden of Gethsemene on a trip to the Holy Land, 1984.

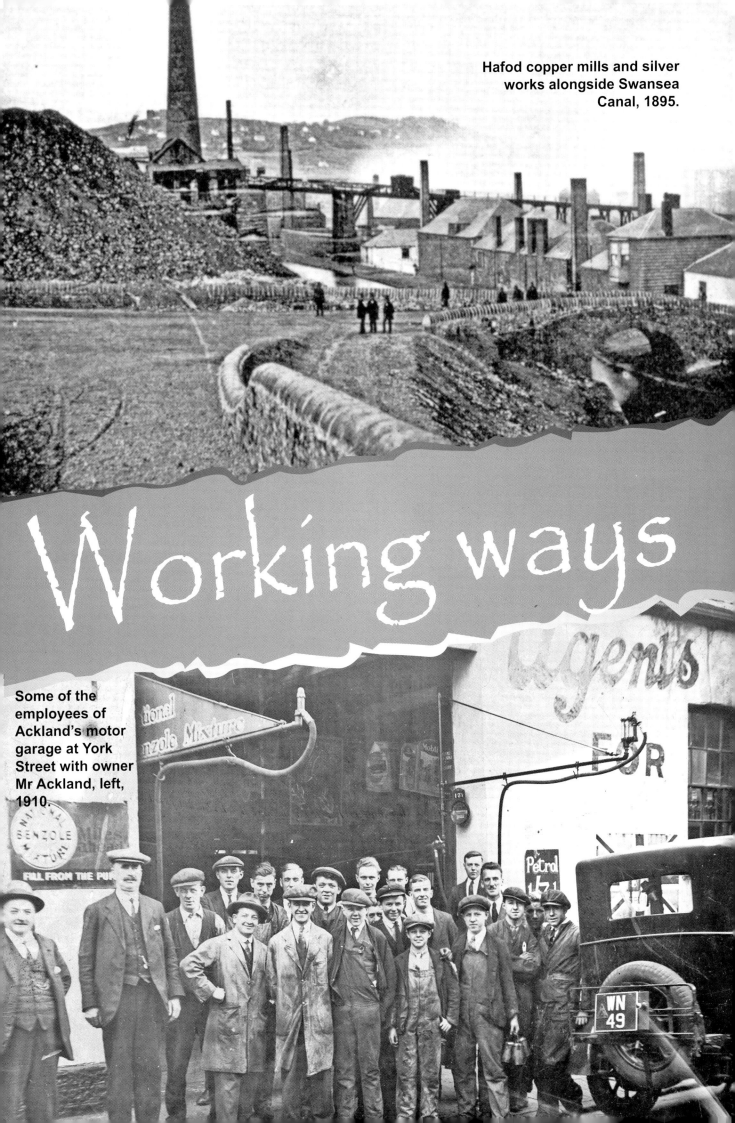

Hafod copper mills and silver works alongside Swansea Canal, 1895.

Working ways

Some of the employees of Ackland's motor garage at York Street with owner Mr Ackland, left, 1910.

A Swansea police sergeant and a woman police officer at The Slip, late 1950s.

Staff of the TJ Rice bakery outside their Gower Road, Sketty, premises, 1957.

Some of the women who worked at Hodges Menswear factory, Fforestfach, 1949.

Cockle gathering women at Penclawdd, carry the fruits of a backbreaking day's labour up from the nearby marshes, 1902.

Builders take a break from their labour during refurbishment of Manselton School, 1954.

Staff of British Home Stores on the opening day of the company's store at Oxford Street, May 1957.

Staff of Macfisheries, Portland Street, 1958.

Youngsters at work in the time office at Richard Thomas & Baldwin's Bryngwyn Tinplate Works in Gorseinon, 1952.

The busy despatch office of the British Road Services North Dock depot, 1961.

Local farmers outside Crws Farm, Three Crosses, waiting for a Milk Marketing Board lorry to collect their churns in 1955. They are, from left: Newton Rees, Heol Las Farm, Blue Anchor, Penclawdd; Alwyn Davies, Cwm Mawr Isaf Farm, Cae Mansel, Gowerton; Glyn Evans, Trecethin Farm, Blue Anchor, Penclawdd; Eric Evans, Gellyeithrym Farm, Gowerton;, Ian Jones, Alltwen Farm, Cae Mansel, Gowerton and Myrddin Gronow, Bryn Hir Farm, Blue Anchor, Penclawdd.

Busy linotype operators at the South Wales Evening Post, Adelaide Street, 1968.

Stage hands with entertainer Stan Stennet, far right, at the Grand Theatre during the pantomime Mother Goose, 1961.

South Wales Transport signwriter Gareth Davies, painting a bus to commemorate Swansea's elevation to city status, 1969.

Lorry drivers in front of some of their vehicles at the North Dock lorry depot of British Road Services, 1961.

Radio DJ Clive Saddington at his console in the Swansea Sound studio. He broadcast for the station for many years during the 1970s.

Averil Davies and Veronica Bateman at the Hodges Menswear factory, Fforestfach, mid-1980s.

The headteacher and staff of Townhill Infants School, 1970.

Lord Mayor of Swansea, Councillor Alan Lloyd, with other civic dignitaries and leading industrialists at the official opening of Swansea Enterprise Zone, 1980.

Looking down at the loading bay of the Corgi toy factory warehouse, Fforestfach,1985.

Staff at the Crymlyn Burrows Freightliner terminal gathered in one of the offices after they had received their severance pay on the day it closed, 1987.

Caravans near the beach at Porteynon, 1967.

Mumbles&Gower

An idyllic rural scene at Fairwood, August 1963.

Langland Bay, with just a glimpse of Rotherslade and the Osborne Hotel, 1907.

Clark's tearooms, Oxwich, 1910. They provided welcome refreshment for many visitors to the area for many years.

Coxswain Billy Gibbs and the crew of the Porteynon lifeboat Janet, during a practice launch. The vessel saw service from 1906-1916.

Camping on the dunes at Three Cliffs Bay, Gower, 1920.

Tut Head, Mumbles was a magnet for walkers in the early 1900s. The pathway at the bottom of the picture led to and from the pier.

Pedestrians make way for a car heading down through the cutting at Mumbles, 1920.

One of two bungalows constructed by Stanley Hinton at Smolden's Field, off Plunch Lane, Limeslade in 1921. He is pictured with members of his family in front of the property.

The sands and beachside houses at Horton, 1935.

The Church and Glebe House, Cheriton, 1935.

A breathtaking view of Caswell Bay, Gower, late 1940s.

Some of the exhibitors and visitors who attended the Gower Show at Penrice, 1938.

Porteynon Bay, late 1940s.

The concrete shelter at Rotherslade Bay, Langland, 1948.

Youngsters enjoying their French loaves at Burrows caravan site, Porteynon, 1958.

A sweeping view of Rhossili Bay and Worms Head, 1972.

A tranquil view of Parkmill, 1955.

A Sunday scene at Southend, August 1967.

La Parisienne, opposite the park, Southend, 1974.

A pleasure boat steams off
from Mumbles Pier, July 1971.

This is the esplanade that replaced the concrete shelter at Rotherslade Bay, Gower, 2000.

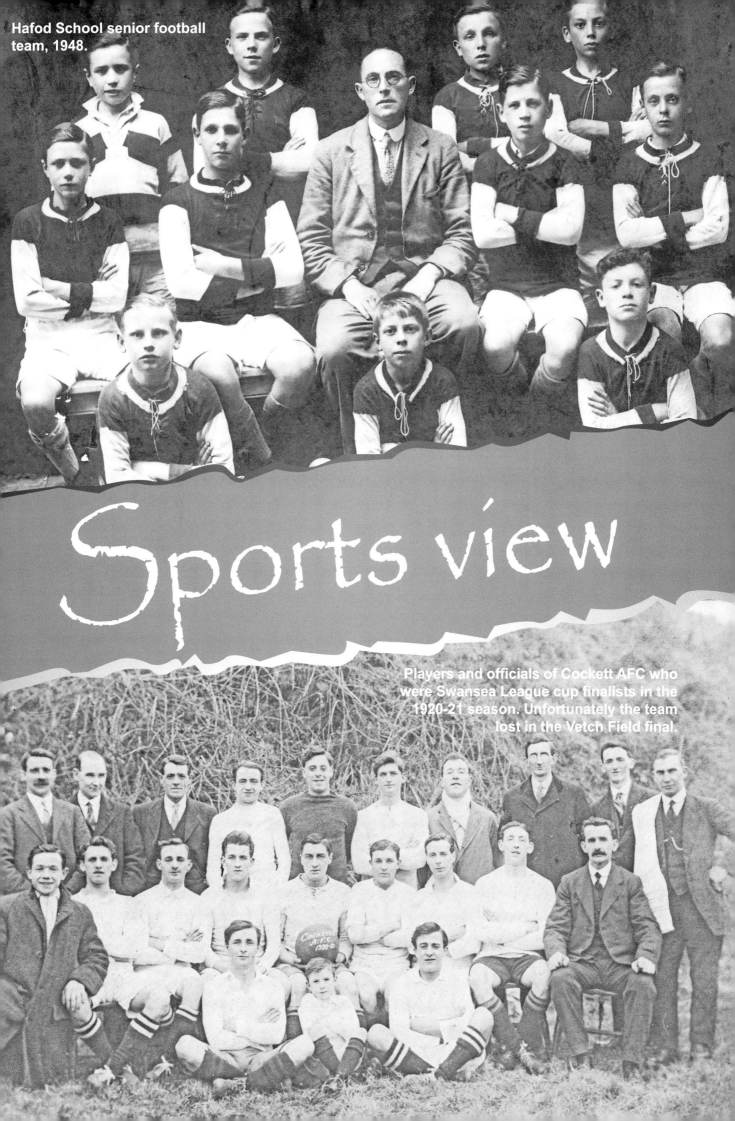

Hafod School senior football team, 1948.

Sports view

Players and officials of Cockett AFC who were Swansea League cup finalists in the 1920-21 season. Unfortunately the team lost in the Vetch Field final.

Members and officials of a Swansea Town football team during a game at Vetch Field, late 1930s.

Young supporters of the successful Swansea Schoolboys soccer team outside Vetch field before watching them play Birmingham team Aston there, 1947.

Swansea Grammar School rugby XV, 1947- 48.

Officials of Kilvey AFC present a portrait to John Jones at a special evening at St Thomas Community Centre in recognition of his sporting achievements, Thursday, June 24, 1948.

Morriston RFC players and officials, 1957.

Swansea Town Cricket Club members, 1952.

The darts team of the Cockett Inn, 1955.

Members of the bowls team of the Richard Thomas & Baldwin's Landore works, 1956. They were semi finalists in the company's West Wales area competition that year.

Swansea's It's A Knock Out team after winning the British heat that was held at St Helen's sports ground in the city, 1975.

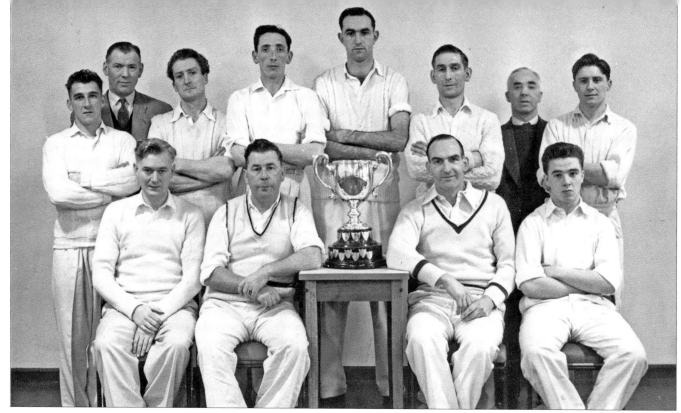

Members of the Station Inn cricket team, St Thomas, who were East Side Cricket League Champions, early 1950s.

Brynhyfryd School pupils after taking part in a schools cricket final at Ashleigh Road playing fields, 1957.

An impressive line up of Swansea Schoolboys who attained their caps for Wales between 1948 and 1958.The middle row of men were all teachers who gave their time to run the Swansea Schools' Saturday League.

Bishop Gore School athletics team with teacher DL Walters 1956-57.

Penlan School Senior B Rugby team, 1959.

Port Tennant Stars, players and officials, at Ashleigh Road, late 1950s.

184

Swansea snooker player Trevor Davies after playing against World Champion Terry Griffiths, at the Cwmfelin Club, November 1979.

The Parkmill Rangers FC team which played in Swansea Senior League Division 7, 1961.

Members of Swansea's British Telecom soccer team with coach Andy Anderson, 1963.

Winch Wen AFC 1962-63.

Penlan School senior soccer team, who were Senior League winners, 1963-64. No fewer than six members of the winning side went on to play for Swansea Schoolboys Welsh Shield winning team.

Terrace Road Junior Mixed School rugby XV, 1963.

Swansea Schools Cricket XI players getting their caps after playing for Wales, 1969. Included in the line up are Glamorgan wicket keeper Alan Jones and bowler Don Shepherd.

A member of Terrace Road Chapel Men's Guild enjoys a game of billiards, 1968.

Swansea Town goalkeeper George Hayes makes a penalty save during a game at the Vetch Field in the club's 1965-66 season.

Members of the Swansea team which won the UK heat of It's A Knockout at St Helen's sports ground, 1975. City singing star Bonnie Tyler is in the front row.

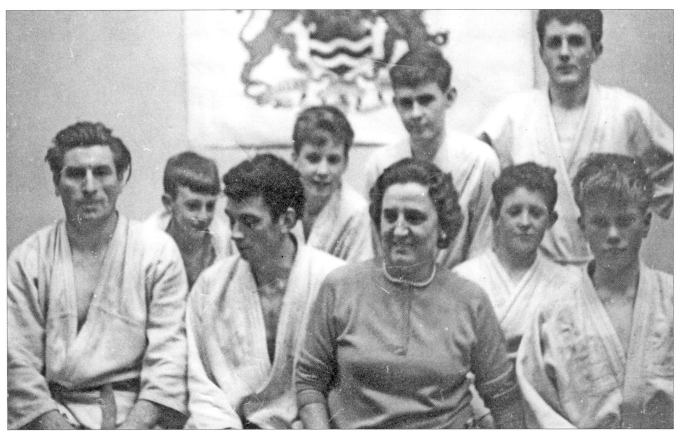

Members and officials of West Cross Judo Club, 1969.

Presentation time for members of the BT Swansea Golf Society after a tournament at Tenby, 1985.

Olchfa Comprehensive School junior girls netball team, 1990.

Award recipients proudly show off their certificates at a presentation evening organised by Swansea Acrobatic Club, October 2000.

Also published by
Bryngold Books
www.bryngoldbooks.com

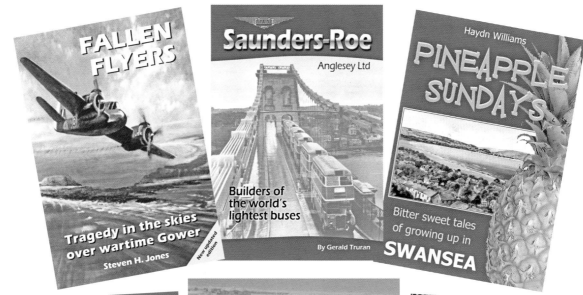

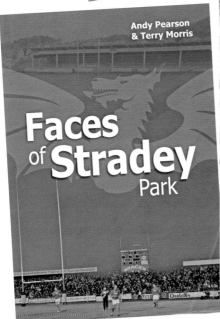

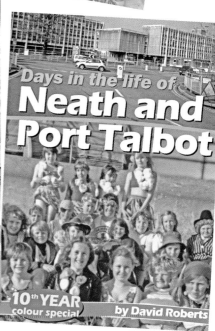

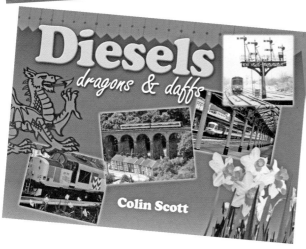

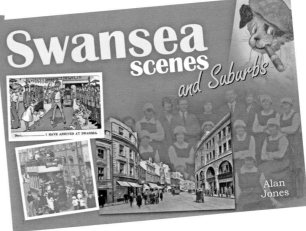

To purchase any of these titles tel: 01639 643961 or email: bryngold@btinternt.com